Trains

Maggie Fischer

Contents

All Aboard!

Some trains move people from one place to another.

All Aboard!

Other trains move large shipments.
These large shipments are called **cargo**.

Parts of a Train

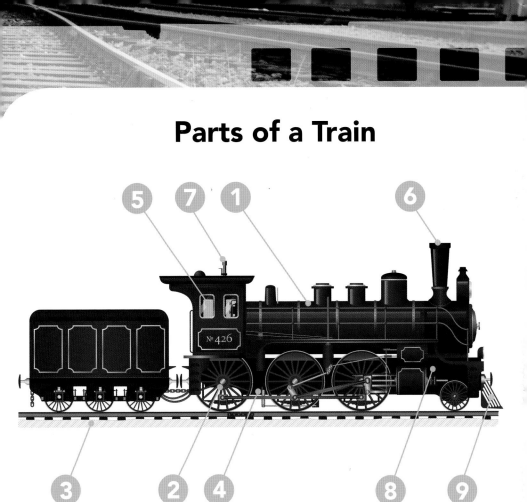

1. engine
2. wheels
3. rail
4. fuel tank
5. cab
6. smokestack
7. warning bell
8. steam chest
9. **cowcatcher** (cattle catcher)

Early Trains

Trains were first pulled by mules, oxen, or horses.
They were designed to pull freight, or heavy loads, long distances.

Early Trains

Trains run along tracks called rails. Special wheels were built to keep the train speeding along the track.

Steam Engines

The first **locomotives**, or engines, were powered by steam.

Burning coal or wood heats water in the engine.

Very hot water creates steam. The steam powers the engine to pull the train.

Passenger Trains

Passenger trains carry people.

The passenger cars are called coaches or carriages.

Today, you can ride in a sleeping car and eat in a dining car.

Freight Trains

Freight trains carry lots of different goods.

Boxcars are big containers on wheels. They can carry boxes, grain, and animals.

A **hopper car** carries coal across the country.

Electric Locomotives

Electric locomotives are powered by a third electric rail or track, by an overhead line, or by batteries.

Electric trains are faster than steam engines.

Electric trains use less fuel than steam engines and do not pollute the air.

Electric Locomotives

Electric locomotives are used to transport people.

Big cities such as New York City and London have electric train systems. They are called **subways**.

Most subways run underground.

Diesel Engines

Diesel engines use oil for **fuel** instead of coal.

Oil is very **flammable**.

It is easily set on fire.

Diesel locomotives can work longer
and run faster than steam engines.

Diesel Engines

Diesel engines are often used to move other train cars on the track.

These diesel locomotives are called **switchers.**

High-Speed Rails and Monorails

High-speed rails are very fast.

Some high-speed rail trains can travel over one hundred miles per hour.

High-speed rails carry passengers.

High-Speed Rails and Monorails

The fastest trains in the world are monorails.

A monorail runs on one track instead of two.

Monorails can travel over three hundred miles per hour.

Ride the Rails

Trains help us get where we need to go!

Trains move people and goods every day.

What is your favorite type of train?

Trains QUIZ

1. What kind of train uses only one rail?
   a) Steam engine
   b) Diesel locomotive
   c) Monorail

2. What were early trains *not* pulled by?
   a) People
   b) Cattle
   c) Horses

3. What kind of trains are used to move other cars around the track?
   a) High-speed rails
   b) Electric locomotives
   c) Switchers

4. What do high-speed trains carry?
   a) Passengers
   b) Food
   c) Livestock

5. What are the tracks that the train wheels sit on called?
   a) Roads
   b) Paths
   c) Rails

6. Which of these cities has a subway system?
   a) San Diego, California
   b) Columbus, Ohio
   c) New York City, New York

GLOSSARY

Boxcar: large containers to carry goods

Cargo: goods or materials carried on trains

Cowcatcher: a device at the front of a train to push cattle out of the way

Flammable: catches on fire easily

Fuel: material that is burned to create power

Hopper car: a type of freight car used to transport coal or grain

Locomotive: a vehicle or machine that travels by rail

Subways: underground electric locomotive system

Switchers: powerful trains that move other trains around the tracks

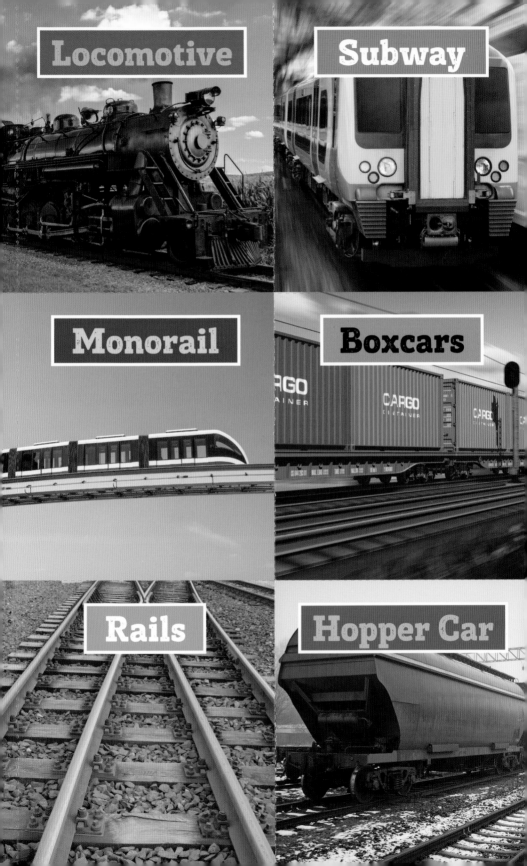

Locomotive

Subway

Monorail

Boxcars

Rails

Hopper Car

A subway is an electric train. It runs underground.

Locomotives are engines powered by steam.

Boxcars are big containers on wheels.

A monorail is the fastest type of train. It runs on one track.

Hopper cars carry coal across the country.

Rails are the tracks that trains ride on.